CH00793466

NORIAKI

Endre Ruset is a poet, literary critic and translator from Molde, Norway. His previous collections include *Kims lek*, ('Kim's Game' Gyldendal, 2005) and *Elsket og savnet*, ('Loved and missed' Kolon, 2014). He has been awarded a Bjørnson Scholarship and the prestigious Bookkeeper Scholarship (2015). He has also been nominated for a Bastian Award for Translation and his latest book, *Deretter* (Flamme Forlag, 2021) co-authored with Harry Man, was a *Dagblaget* Book of the Year.

Harry Man's *Lift* (Tall Lighthouse, 2014) won the UNESCO Bridges of Struga Award. His second pamphlet, *Finders Keepers*, was shortlisted for the Ted Hughes Award for New Work in Poetry. His co-collection, authored with Endre Ruset, *Deretter* ('Thereafter', Flamme Forlag, 2021) won the Stephen Spender Prize. He was shortlisted for Tees Valley Artist of the Year 2024. His first collection *Popular Song* (2024) was published by Nine Arches Press. He lives in County Durham.

Also by Endre Ruset

Utøya Thereafter: *Poems in Memory of the 2011 Norway Attacks*	(Hercules Editions, 2021)
Deretter	(Flamme Forlag, 2021)
Elsket og savnet	(Gyldendal, 2014)
Kims lek	(Gyldendal, 2005)
Ribbeinas vingespenn	(Gyldendal, 2001)

Also by Harry Man

Popular Song	(Nine Arches Press, 2024)
Utøya Thereafter: *Poems in Memory of the 2011 Norway Attacks*	(Hercules Editions, 2021)
Deretter	(Flamme Forlag, 2021)
Greatist Hits II: *Selected Collaborations of SJ Fowler and Harry Man*	(Kingston University Press, 2019)
Finders Keepers	(Sidekick Books, 2016)
Lift	(Tall Lighthouse, 2013)

CONTENTS

This translation has been published
with the financial support of NORLA

NORLA
Norwegian
Literature Abroad

ISBN: 978-1-916938-51-9

Cover designed by Aaron Kent

Typeset by Aaron Kent

Broken Sleep Books Ltd
PO BOX 102
Llandysul
SA44 9BG

Noriaki

Endre Ruset
Translated by Harry Man

Broken Sleep Books

FOREWORD

There is a popular, fanciful notion that there's a short, straight line from ski jumping to the psych ward, drug addiction, poetry and early death. That the sport is reserved for the exceptional. Not for what they possess, but for what they lack. They lack the fear, the rational risk assessment and self-preservation instinct that makes the rest of us choose the role of the shivering spectator. This while they, the ski jumpers, choose the uplift off the face of the hill, the capricious airflows of fate that in the blink of an eye can counteract gravity and make a frail human on two skis soar like a god.

Most Norwegians have tried ski jumping. On smaller, then slightly larger hills. But at a fairly early stage, reason has prevailed and we've switched to become spectators instead. Ski jumping is an escape from the mundane, an arena in which everyone can use their imagination and dream of weightlessness and find themselves in harmony with the forces of nature and – on a good day – after a successful landing, the resounding roar of the crowd.

A decent jump can last, say, eight seconds. The ski jumper must express themselves in those seconds. It's a fine art.

— Jo Nesbø

At the launch bar, the athlete must face a vertiginous, Gulliver-like new view of the world. Spectators, now giddyingly small, appear more like crumbs in an overturned toaster tray, spilling out on the gleaming linoleum of snow. Two astronautic heads, the live view of the athlete themselves swim on fairylight-like Sony screens. The scaffold of the in-run rattles. The flagpoles rattle. Under the drip of the snow, the ground creaks like the deck of a ship. In the foreground is a dot matrix display with the windspeed in kilometres per hour, miles per hour, a countdown for the skier to lift their body into position, to push off, and underneath, TIMEX in thick, intimidating type.

At the height of the large hill, the wind whips around as the nervous breaths of different countries' medical teams and coaches cross through the floodlights. Here the athlete will wait for a ruling on the windspeed. If the windspeed is too fast, the International Skiing Federation (FIS) will put the entire competition on hold. If the speed is too fast for too long the FIS must cancel the entire event altogether. This critical responsibility used to fall to legendary ski jumping Race Director Walter-Hofer who has only recently handed over his walkie-talkie and trademark red headband to relative newcomer Sandro Pertile.

If all is well, once given the nod, the athlete must edge onto the bar, their warmed and stretched legs sticking to the cold steel, lightly rotate their feet, swing their skis into the specially-designed ceramic aloslide grooves. This action fully commits their form, their weight and focus to an unfinished tightrope bridge from the crest of the hill to somewhere out above the mountain-line, to the roof of the world.

The red light switches to black, to green. The flag drops and the countdown to reach the edge of the jump begins.

The athlete has a sharpness in their mouth as if biting the skin of a satsuma, which is the bitter taste of adrenalin, as the body's somatic, survival instinct kicks in. Ski jumpers speak of a tunnel vision that accompanies the approximately 36 degree incline of the ramp or "in-run". Alternating their bodyweight from one ski to another down the in-run helps to reduce friction and build speed down the long, accelerating scrape. The rush of roaring, compressed, icy wind makes their lycra cup then clasp, then tighten against their bodies as if giving an iceberg a bear hug in the nude. Gravity pulls at their cheeks with a g-force stronger than that experienced by the space shuttle pilots of the past. Knees bent, arms behind them, parallel to the hill, the skier's back straight and head bent up, they must alter their posture to maximise their speed, squeezing their body down to physically resemble as closely as possible the aerodynamic shape of a wind-ferried raindrop. A sensation like trying to kneel down on the roof of a car as it accelerates into the joining lane of the M25. Even beneath wind-tunnel-tested goggles, the eyes produce tears that scroll horizontally along the tensed crow's feet, toward the foam and sweat-salted elastic as the skier's ears pop and their teeth chatter like cups on a trolley. The crashing white noise of air flows across their tightened shoulders and must slip as unresisted from their fingers.

As the skier tops out at around 60 miles an hour, their skis bend up into the scoop and they must be ready to hop or leap. Their movements are like those of a puppeteer ahead of the mechanical extension of their body – their lightweight plastic skis 145% of the skier's own height. At the jump edge they spring off and into the first seconds of a picture-perfect, airborne silence.

*   *   *   *

In Norway ski jumping is perhaps as familiar as a local park's five-a-side to anyone in England. Once ski jumps were ubiquitous in Norway, and reached their heyday in the 1950s and 60s. Upkeep of a ski jump is an expensive and labour-intensive business and over the years many have either been torn down and demolished, or simply abandoned to the elements. A large number sit in the hillside like galvanised, retrofuture monuments that speak to a rosy-cheeked past of the same variety as the wooden toboggan of the Christmas card. Recently photographer Espen Tveit travelled the country taking photographs of the 200 in-runs that still remain. Despite this sense of the loss of times past, this heritage was nevertheless the foundation for a reliably impressive winter sports prestige that remains the envy of the world. Norway beat the USA, Russia and China, bringing home a horde of 37 medals at 2022 Beijing Olympics. They also won 16 golds – twice the number brought home by Team USA, made all the more remarkable by the fact you could fit the entire population of Norway into London and still have two million people left in change. The climate then of these poems is one of both nostalgic attachment to the sport and a deep admiration for ski jumping as an international sport today.

In his trademark yellow jump suit, Noriaki Kasai is a record-obliterating eight time Winter Olympian. At 20 years old Kasai, a native of Simokawa, Japan, competed at the Olympics in Albertville in 1992. After Lillehammer, Nagano and Salt Lake City, Kasai jumped in Turin aged 34 and most recently and perhaps at his last ever Olympics in Pyeongchang in 2018 aged 46. He is polite, reclusive, always speaks well of his competitors and is a role model for aspiring skiers all over the world. To date Noriaki Kasai has won two silver medals and a bronze at the Olympics and has been a Ski Flying World Champion with an incredible seven additional medals to his name in the World Championships from 1999-2015, completing 569 starts across his thirty year career. In 2016 he made the Guinness World Records for "the most appearances in FIS Nordic World Ski Championships by an individual ski jumper" and "the most individual starts in FIS Ski Jumping World Cup competitions". Ever modest, at the time, Kasai said, "When I was a child, I hated losing anytime, anywhere ... When it comes to 'continuing belief' in oneself, it is important for me to have consideration and appreciation for other people – I have many people to thank for my achievement." At the time of writing, it's 2024 and Kasai, aged 52 years old, continues to compete internationally.

Endre Ruset wrote just over 1,500 poems to make this collection, so what we're seeing is the result of a studied narrowing down to arrive at this finished book. There's also a nod to the Norwegian haiku-esque three line poems of Jan Erik Vold's *spor, snø* ("track, snow") that tread the line between lighthearted pun, acutely observed image and social commentary. One of Vold's poems makes an elegant shift from talking about pinecones, to the role of the Norwegian monarchy to a strong inner desire he has to pat the bald head of one of Norway's most admired poets of the 20th Century,

Harald Sverdrup. Similar to playing on different meanings of the word "crown" in English, Vold plays on the pun in Norwegian between "cone" and "king". It's blink-and-you'll-miss-it humour, both playful and rewarding to the reader.

You can see a similar streak in Ruset's poetry, like the deceptively simple haiku that opens "bokfink, høstløv, / Jan Boklöv" which translates to "chaffinch, autumn leaves / Jan Boklöv". Jan Boklöv's trademark V-style, has become the textbook example for ski-jumpers everywhere, allowing skiers to extend their flight. Copying the intricate sounds of Ruset's original poem, we would arrive at something like "dove, autumn above, / Jan Boklöv". The word "bok" here, can also mean "book" and the compound "bokfink" skates pretty close to "book-nicety" and "bookish thinking". Then we're given this final line that translates literally to, "Noriaki hums" or "Noriaki humming". We hear the skis hum, before we see the shape glide through the bird's flightpath and the treetops, yet we're also privy to Noriaki's thoughts, about holding onto the V, the reader is both within Noriaki's mind and watching him mid-flight simultaneously. To do this kind of literary stuntwork in three lines takes serious skill and to translate them a challenge full of risk (and of course, for us as readers there's a thrill there too).

*   *   *   *

The moment the athlete is in the air, they must instantly change their entire body position, spread their stance in the face of the wind, from raindrop to the X of a star jump, forcing their knees to straighten as they roll their legs apart and fight to turn their feet outward and upward as if to kiss the tips of their own skis, leaning like a weather presenter caught in the opening phase of a hurricane. The skier holds open their chest, their body, their jaw, their mouth to the dry, sharp winter air. Here they sail like a dropped tea tray, on a diagonal, make minute adjustments to their position to increase the drag on the body and reduce the speed of their flight, past the concrete block of judges, the iconic Olympic rings and their own shadow rising toward them, toward the emerging ruler's edge of the construction or "K-point" as the true size of the world re-enters the frame of the mind. Here too, a recent addition to the sport becomes visible, a wide, green, laser beam line showing on the out-run where the current leader of the competition has landed. Beyond this line, small, fake plastic fir tree branches help the skier with their depth perception, acting like inverted runway lights.

At this critical second, weightless, the skier must assess the gamble of the touchdown. The change in momentum of an object from high speed flight through air to sudden landing is known as "impulsive force". This force is considered in the testing of air bags, the deceleration of high-speed trains, the telemetry of golf balls, and the configuration of egg boxes. It has been measured in the design of baseball mitts and the effect of boxing gloves on the ribcages and skulls of contenders. In ski jumping, the impulsive force is calculated by taking the total mass of the skier and multiplying it by the change in their velocity. Too much and you risk breaking a shin, shattering an ankle, or spin-washing your body in a powdery rubble of snow. By tilting their skis forward and touching down with the back of the skis first, the jumper can hit the ground at an angle parallel with the downward ramp while minimising any chance of rotation. Landing beyond the K-point, one foot in front of the other, the skier picks up style points. Named after the famous Norwegian region of the same name, this is what is called a "telemarked landing". The use of the angle of the ramp to absorb some of their momentum reduces the impulsive force and safely and gradually allows the skier to reduce their speed as the camera crews run and clamber through clods of snow toward them for a reaction shot, a group in the crowd raising a snow-white teddy bear to the sky.

*   *   *   *

As this book attests, not everything has gone Kasai's way and challenges that skiers face include unpredictable headwinds which can affect buoyancy in the air as well as differing friction down the in-run creating a certain element of chance to the sport. This has led to an increased sense of both camaraderie and frustration among competitors as well as increasing the excitement for its spectators. Kasai himself said at Beijing 2022 that he was now rooting for young athletes and was optimistic that fellow Japanese jumper Ryoyu Kobayashi was in with a chance of winning gold.

He was right.

In writing this book, Endre Ruset has drawn on the work of a broad spectrum of poets, from Matsuo Bashō and Kobayashi Issa to Gertrude Stein, Keats and Wallace Stevens to Robert Creeley and Greek Mythology, using the identifiable three line structure of a haiku as a template for each chart poem. The poems charts the ski jumper's performances from competition to competition, noting his effortful near-misses "Noriaki in fourth place" and Kasai's transformative style and come-back triumphs, "Noriaki a raindrop / in Hakuba / in Harrachov a butterfly".

We're often taught that haiku are written in three lines with a 5-7-5 syllable pattern. To a Western ear, this feels comfortable. Copywriters frequently condense down their sentences to less than 17 syllables. According to a paper published in the *Journal of Speech and Hearing Research* the average human breath will stretch across 16.55 syllables. The haiku seems the perfect vessel for this. Unfortunately the typical view that all haiku must have five syllables then seven then five is based on some shaky ground. While the number of syllables in English typically represents the number of sounds in a word, Japanese uses not only the number, but the time it takes to pronounce that sound (measured by a unit called 'on' in Japanese and 'mora' in English). These come into play with double vowel sounds in words like "broom" or "need" for example, where the double vowel sound means the word contains two morae, but one syllable. Traditionally haiku are written using this system, meaning that it's the morae and not the syllables that should be counted. Add to this that hokku and haiku in Japanese often have no line breaks whatsoever and that they frequently break the number of morae per line too and you can begin to see how much the form has a certain flexibility.

Within the haiku there are other considerations, the originating *haikai* implies a continuation, a sense of humour with a lightness of touch (*karumi* in Japanese). In particular the use of puns and *haigon* or words that could be from another language or that were more demotic, colloquial or everyday were seen as features that lent a certain crudeness to the poems, but also this notion of a lightness of touch. The complexity grows in the form of *kireji* or cutting words or exclamations which work almost like linebreaks, not to mention all manner of other intricate features from *iisute* associated with an ending mid-flow due to an absent poetry collaborator in the case of renga (collaborative haiku sequences) and *kyu* which is used to describe words heard after an enjoyable dinner together and more specifically the fragments of words heard as people say goodbye and disappear off into the night.

As a translator, these poems pose both evident and more discreet challenges. In many ways, given all these considerations, translating a haiku from any language into English successfully is something of a fool's errand, but it speaks to poetry's position of both Don Paterson's assertion that it is "meaning in flight" as well as Bashō's conception of the poem being famously the "narrow road to the interior". Bashō's writing pre-dated the haiku, which is only really a modern conception popularised by Masaoka Shiki (1867 – 1902). This led translator David Barnhill to remark that, "Especially for translations intended for both a scholarly and a general audience, I simply don't think there is a fully satisfactory approach." A perfect sonnet in English is a platonic ideal and poems have a tendency to die on the hill and so part of poetry's gracefulness comes in how it does this while conserving a continuing momentum into the mythic and transcendent. When reading these poems for the first time, I was in two minds about it too – the tradition of ski jumping, the humour, the seasons, the words and phrases heard in the mountains that would arrive and once through UK customs, go through their pockets and discover they'd been robbed of any currency that would let them travel further. From Norwegian Bokmål, English feels cluttered with its need for apostrophes and appropriate indefinite articles and the present continuous tense. I've adopted Endre Ruset's use of the lowercase and punctuation, which is all in an effort to conserve the feeling of the original as far as possible. In Norwegian, the language itself is more Germanic and self-contained, offering different options to distil the language down to its sparest form. Where Noriaki leaps across the face of the moon, Ruset's language has a double meaning, "raus Noriaki", pulling on the adopted German "raus" of encouragement on the slopes, as well as the Norwegian word for "generous". The poem in the original reads, "raus Noriaki / signerer ansiktet / til månen" literally "[*raus* / generous] Noriaki / [is signing / signs] [the face / a face / face] / of [the moon / a moon / moon]" which loses the note of contemplative respect for the athlete taking time to sign autographs for fans and to treat them to his style and flair in his gravity-defying jumps as well as a sense of the trajectory of Noriaki Kasai's spirited flight through the air. I've had to make choices throughout the translation to take care to prioritise literal meaning, to carry across from one language to another the goodwill, the charisma and humour, the energy and of course the inner magnetic pull of the sport – all of which is present so vividly in the original. The V-shape across pages moving up and down is faithful to the original internal designs by Yokoland in Norway, a visual imitation of the highs and lows, as well as the Jan Boklöv V-style shape of ski-jumping.

If, like me, you're something of a newcomer to ski jumping, as well as this introduction, I've done my best to provide a small set of notes in the back, pointing to individual competitions, technical ski-jumping terminology and other details that I sometimes had to set to one side in the translation in favour of this feeling of *haigon,* pun and playfulness. Some poems read more like three loosely connected statements that recall terms from *saijiki* (season dictionaries) in which haikai poets agreed upon certain terms that epitomised one season or another offering different meanings as you skip from the first line to the last. Additionally, Noriaki's name slips from the first, to the second, to the third line throughout.

In Norway this book is now available as a record, with Endre Ruset reading the poems accompanied by a warm and effortlessly stylish jazz and electronica backing from Jon Balke and Stian Omenås that I heartily recommend. Ruset himself commented recently, on the poems that they "spring out of ski jumping but are primarily about life. The happy, the sad, the heavy, the fresh, the light, the dark. Out from the jumping hill and into mythology."

— Harry Man
UK 2024

Til Nori

For Nori

Noriaki på
bommen, gul drakt
i år også

Noriaki on
the launch bar, gold suits
this year too

første snøfall
Noriaki våkner
himmelen blomstrer

first snow
Noriaki wakes
the sky blossoms

der hoppkanten
slutter, begynner
Noriaki

there the jump's edge
ending, beginning
Noriaki

*

Noriaki stille
som en knokkel
over kulen

Noriaki quiet
as the white knuckle
of the hill

*

regn over Sanru-elva
Noriaki fisker
kirsebærørret

rain over the Sanru river
Noriaki fly-fishes
cherry trout

*

hoppbakken i
Shimokawa, dufter av
Noriakis barndom

the flying hill in
Shimokawa, hints of
Noriaki's childhood

*

*

raus Noriaki
signerer ansiktet
til månen

generous Noriaki
signs the face
of the moon

*

himmelen spenner
buen, Noriaki
blir en pil

the sky opens
the bow, Noriaki
the arrow

*

i sommerhuset
under en vinterfrakk
Noriaki sovende

in a summer house
under a winter coat
Noriaki sleeps

*

*

Noriaki
en fugleunge
før sitt første hopp

Noriaki
a baby bird
before his first leap

*

mens vi venter på
Noriaki, hopper
Godot bakken ned

while we wait for
Noriaki, having gone
Godot is ground down

*

i Engelbergtluft
som mørkner
flyr Noriaki

in Engelberg air
darkening
flying Noriaki

*

*

Noriaki født
Hokkaidonatta
gul og svart

Noriaki christening
Hokkaido night
yellow and black

*

hørte
du? Noriaki
som falt

caught
wind? Noriaki
falls

*

kort dag, kjølig blå
en strofe bærer
Noriaki til seier

short day, cold blue
a strophe bears
Noriaki to glory

*

*

Noriaki venter
fem sekundmeter
Walter Hofer-blues

Noriaki awaits
the wind speed ruling
Walter Hofer-blues

*

innerst i stillheten
sitter Noriaki med
vinternotatene

innermost silence
sits with Noriaki
season notes of winter

*

vesle japanjernspurv!
vesle kizukispett!
vesle Noriaki!

little japanese iron sparrow!
little kuzuki woodpecker!
little Noriaki!

*

Noriaki finner
endelig et svev
som bærer

Noriaki at last
finds a float
some bearing

*

Zakopane
Noriaki og en kjøttmeis
på bommen

Zakopane
Noriaki and a titmouse
by the launch bar

*

riskorn for riskorn
tetner himmelen
rundt Noriaki

rice grain by rice grain
swilling sky
around Noriaki

*

*

Noriaki tårer
regndråper
i østavind

Noriaki tears
raindrops
in the East wind

*

rød, lettsaltet himmel
Noriaki spiser
makrellskyer i tomat

red, lightly seasoned heaven
Noriaki swallows
mackerel clouds in tomato dressing

*

19 18,5 19
18,5 18
Noriaki på fjerde

19 18.5 19
18.5 18
Noriaki comes fourth

*

*

forelsket Noriaki
svever opp trappene
flyr bakken ned

in love Noriaki
soars up stairs
flies back down

*

hopp!
Noriaki
hopp!

jump!
Noriaki
jump!

*

raggsokkdiskotek
i kjellerstua
(Noriakis bursdag, 9 år)

raggsock disco party
in the basement
(Noriaki's birthday, aged 9)

*

*

Noriaki utspent
et klesplagg til tørk
blafrer i vinden

Noriaki outstretched
washing
flutters in the wind

*

vinterkysset
Noriakis kinn
en isende flekk

winter's kissed
Noriaki's chin
a spot of ice

*

bokfink, høstløv
Jan Boklöv
nynner Noriaki

chaffinch, autumn leaves
Jan Boklöv
hum of Noriaki

*

*

Noriaki følger
et gaupespor
til verdens ende

Noriaki follows
the trail of a bobcat
to the end of the world

*

først lyden
så Noriaki
så himmelen

first the sound
then Noriaki
then the sky

*

syv kameler
to esler
delvis Noriaki

seven camels
two donkeys
one part Noriaki

*

*

Noriaki
henger der
ikke

Noriaki
hangs about
no longer

*

dress er jobbantrekk
i sivil går Noriaki
silkeveien

dressed for work
casual Noriaki
takes the silk road

*

fuglene flyr fra
fugletapetet, inn
i Noriakis drøm

birds fly from
bird wallpaper, irrupt
into Noriaki's dream

*

*

Noriaki er regndråpe
i Hakuba
sommerfugl i Harrachov

Noriaki a raindrop
in Hakuba
in Harrachov a butterfly

*

nedsnødd unnarenn
Noriaki på rygg
lager snøengel

snow covers the out-run
Noriaki back to the snow
makes an angel

*

det første hoppet
det første kysset
Noriaki vektløs

the first leap
the first kiss
Noriaki weightless

*

*

Noriakis nedslag
blir
min barndom

Noriaki's impact
becoming
my childhood

*

vindvimplene visner
Noriaki slår skiene
ut i blomst

the wind flags wilt
Noriaki hits the skis
blossoms

*

Dire Straits
på bilstereoen
smooth Noriaki

Dire Straits
on the car stereo
smooth Noriaki

*

Noriaki lytter
til Japanhavet
i en medbrakt konkylie

Noriaki listens
to the Sea of Japan
he brought along a conch shell

*

ensomt høstløv
Noriaki går rundt
i et Kulm-vindkast

lone autumn leaf
Noriaki goes around
in the Kulm gust

*

en rose er en rose
er en frostrose
på Noriakis briller

a rose is a rose
is a frozen rose
on the glasses of Noriaki

*

*

Noriaki
og skyggen av Noriaki
i nedslaget

Noriaki
and the shadow Noriaki
impact

*

gjennomsiktig
Noriaki på ei lang
hvit bro

seeing through
Noriaki by one long
white bridge

*

latteren
til jenta
Noriaki liker

laughter
for a girl
Noriaki's liking

*

alt er Noriaki
om du ser
lenge nok

everything is Noriaki
if you look
long enough

*

sikker på seier
gjør Noriaki V-
tegn med skiene

confident of victory
Noriaki makes a V-
shape with his skis

*

gutten i tårnet
mannen i svevet
Noriaki

the boy in the tower
the man on the wing
Noriaki

*

*

Noriaki
og en brunstig tiur
måler krefter

Noriaki
and a wood grouse in heat
measure up

*

kom nærmere!
roper Noriaki
til k-punktet

come closer!
Noriaki exclaims
to the K-point

*

halvmånen likner
et ovarenn
Noriaki tar sats

crescent moon-like
an in-run
Noriaki takes a bet

*

Noriaki ser
et ekorn med pingpong-
ball i kjeften

Noriaki looks
a squirrel with a ping-pong
ball in the mouth

*

fullmåneskinn
gul Noriaki
kveldsrenn Kuusamo

full moon
yellow Noriaki
evening competition Kuusamo

*

en hel vinter
danser grankonglene
for Noriaki

all winter long
pine cones dance
for Noriaki

*

*

Noriaki må nok
ned mot 130
skal han klare det

Noriaki probably
needs a 130
to make it

*

taus karaokebar
Noriaki alene
innerste bordet

silent karaoke bar
Noriaki alone
centre table

*

Funaki, Harada,
Okabe, Saitō, Kasaya
siden Noriaki

Funaki, Harada,
Okabe, Saitō, Kasaya
since Noriaki

*

*

Noriaki ber
om unnskyldning
til den fine oppdriften

Noriaki implores
forgiveness
for the fine uplift

*

bryllupsnatt
Noriaki lander
på g-punktet

wedding night
Noriaki landing
the g-spot

*

origamiblomst
ned ei stille elv
Noriaki flyr

origami flower
down a still river
Noriaki floating

*

her svever Noriaki
hvis navn
står skrevet i luft

here flies Noriaki
whose name
is writ in air

alt som beveger seg
Noriaki
i svarttrostens øye

all the things moving
Noriaki
in the blackbird's eye

snøen faller
som regn
Noriaki smelter

snow falling
like rain
Noriaki melts away

*

Noriaki gjemt
et sølvskjåer
i skyene

Noriaki hiding
a silver lining
in the clouds

*

sommernatt i Sapporo
Noriaki drømmer
om vinter i Kollen

summer night in Sapporo
Noriaki dreams about
winter in Kollen

*

på hoppukas
syvende dag
våkner Noriaki

Ski Jumping Week
seventh day
Noriaki wakes up

*

*

Noriaki & Noriaki
& Noriaki & Noriaki
i speillabyrinten

Noriaki & Noriaki
& Noriaki & Noriaki
in a hall of mirrors

*

i et tidels sekund
tas Noriaki til fange
i en dråpe dugg

for a split second
Noriaki taken prisoner
in a dewdrop

*

gnist for gnist
daler snøen
på Noriakis hjerte

spark by spark
a vale of snow
at Noriaki's heart

*

*

Noriaki letter
skituppene
gnistrer

Noriaki eases off
ski tips
sparkling

*

lille flammesover
Noriaki
når våkner du?

little sleeping flame
Noriaki
when will you reawaken?

*

vårkrokusene
i Harrachov vet ikke
hvem Noriaki er

crocus flowers in spring
unknown in Harrachov
who Noriaki is

*

*

grønn Noriaki
rød Noriaki
ingen Noriaki

green Noriaki
red Noriaki
gone Noriaki

*

Kurosawa regisserer
Noriaki fra urnen
i Anyo-Ji

Kurosawa directing
Noriaki from the ashes
in Anyo-Ji

*

kirkeklokka
i Vikersund ringer
for Noriaki

church bells
in Vikersund ring
for Noriaki

*

*

munter Noriaki
danser robotdans
for rekruttene

cheerful Noriaki
robot dances
for recruits

*

lyskasterne slukner
Noriaki
lyser

spotlights out
Noriaki
lit up

*

et snøfnugg er
hodeplagg nok
for Noriakis fingertupp

snow fluff
sufficient headgear
for Noriaki's fingertip

*

*

Noriaki holder
tamagotchien i live
i 36 døgn

Noriaki keeping
the Tamagotchi alive
some 36 days

*

kostymefest
Noriaki utkledd
som tordivel

fancy dress
Noriaki's costume
a daredevil

*

det store gjøkuret
i Bischofshofen
Noriaki ko-ko

the great cuckoo clock
in Bischofshofen
Noriaki cuckoo

*

*

Noriaki spiser
svarte sitroner
til frokost

Noriaki eating
dried limes
at breakfast

*

vindkorridoren
Noriaki
holder pusten

wind corridor
Noriaki
holding breaths

*

hoppkanten
finnes ikke
hopp Noriaki!

the lip of the jump
does not exist
jump Noriaki!

*

*

Noriaki
spiller yatzi med
himmelblå terninger

Noriaki
playing Yatzy with
sky blue dice

*

gammel dame
Noriaki hopper
plakk!

grand dame
Noriaki leaps
phew!

*

tulipanbiene
i Toyoma
svermer for Noriaki

tulips
in Toyoma
swarms for Noriaki

*

*

Noriaki!
livet har ingen utside
alle hopp er eksamen

Noriaki!
outside life is nothing
all jumps are exams

*

17 luftige
stavelser; Noriaki
diktet av Issa

lofty 17
syllables; Noriaki
Issa's poetry

*

den finske døden
åt snø i høyden
mimrer Noriaki

Finnish death
eating snow at high altitude
Noriaki remembers

*

*

Noriaki ser
atten øyenbryn
i skyene

Noriaki spots
eighteen eyebrows
in the skies

*

snøfnugg til snøfnugg
klatrer Noriaki
opp himmelen

snowflake by snowflake
Noriaki climbing
up to the sky

*

fra bunnen av
Hornindalsvatnet tar
Noriaki sats

from the bottom of
Lake Hornindal places
Noriaki bets

*

*

Noriaki
alene
i jubelbruset

Noriaki
alone
in the roar of celebration

*

nytt hotellrom
Noriaki småprater
med fjernkontrollen

new hotel room
Noriaki small talk
with the remote

*

vinden blåser
i det siste løvet
Noriaki blir sittende

wind ushers
in the last leaf
Noriaki settled down

*

*

Noriaki var her
mens vi sov
han vekket oss ikke

Noriaki was here
as we slept
he did not wake us

*

Mühlenkopfschanze
Noriaki bretter
papirfly

Mühlenkopfschanze
Noriaki folds
paper aeroplanes

*

alene, nord
i akebakken
Noriaki

alone, north
on the sledging hill
Noriaki

*

*

mellom Noriaki
den yngre og eldre
22 000 svev

between Noriaki
the young and the old
leap 22,000

*

葛西 紀明
Noriaki skriver
18 autografer

葛西 紀明
Noriaki's characterful
18 autographs

*

Hokusai
glemte han å
male Noriaki?

Hokusai
did he forget
painting Noriaki?

*

*

Noriaki hopper
ut av senga
3x18

Noriaki jumps
out of bed
3 x 18

*

ved foten av fjellet
Noriaki
på snøorgel

at the foot of the mountain
Noriaki
the snow stadium's organ

*

tåke rundt tårnet
tåke i bakken
Noriakis frostlepper

mist around the tower
mist along the ground
Noriaki's frozen lip

*

*

Noriaki mister
trykket på
høyre ski

Noriaki losing
pressure on
right ski

*

sol og måne
samtidig; Noriakis
søstre smiler

sun and moon
coinciding; Noriaki's
sisters smiling

*

vinterhalvåret
stiller klokka
etter Noriaki

winter season
clocks go back
after Noriaki

*

*

Noriaki venter
på stillkarakterer
ennå skjelver skiene

Noriaki waits
for silent characters
shivering skis

*

sola går ned
med ei stripe Noriaki
etter seg

the sun slips down
a streak of Noriaki
in its wake

*

gjennom syv
samuraier
flyr Noriaki

through seven
samurai
Noriaki flies

*

*

skuffet Noriaki
på vei inn i brakka
snøugleansikt

disappointed Noriaki
on his way through the barricades
the face of a snowy owl

*

for hver seier
blir Noriaki
litt mindre

with every win
Noriaki remains
little smaller

*

sola brenner
gjennom brystet
ditt Noriaki

the sun burns
through your chest
Noriaki

*

*

Noriaki
kjefter opp
vinterskogen

Noriaki
shouts down
the winter forest

*

en vinterreisende
Noriaki alene
i Innsbruck

winter travelling
Noriaki alone
in Innsbruck

*

nord, sør, øst, vest
i midten
flyr Noriaki

north, south, east, west
through the middle
Noriaki flights

*

*

etter Noriaki
omriss av himmel
rester av svev

after Noriaki
the sky's outline
soaring remains

*

sesongslutt i Planica
Noriaki folder
vingene sammen

season's end in Planica
Noriaki folds
wings up

*

kirsebærtreet blomstrer
furua står og ser på
Noriaki nøytral

cherry blossoms
pine standing and overlooking
neutral Noriaki

*

Noriaki skriker
med istidens utdødde
stemme

Noriaki cries
the Ice Age extinction
voiced

*

gode år hagler
Noriaki-sekunder
lette vekter, tunge fjær

good years hail
Noriaki-seconds
weigh light, spring ample

*

skolens nest peneste
sølv i OL
Noriaki mimrer

school pretty second
silver at the Olympics
Noriaki remembers

*

*

på Noriakis
skuldre faller snøen
som rulletekst

by Noriaki
snow falling on his shoulders
scrolling texts

*

bortenfor bakken
flyter Noriaki
sovende på vinden

off the hill
Noriaki in flow
sleeps in the wind

*

nettene vokser
nedover anklene
til Noriaki

nights grow
clean down to the ankles
for Noriaki

*

Noriakis gamle
hoppdress; fugleskremsel
i risåkeren

Noriaki's retired
jump suit; scarecrow
in the rice field

himmelen visner
Noriakis eldes
knær og måne skjelver

sky wrinkling
Noriaki's aging
knees and moon tremble

av alle gule blader
som faller mot snøen
er Noriaki det vakreste

among all the yellow leaves
falling against the snow
Noriaki is the most beautiful

NOTES

launch bar: In ski jumping, the launch bar is called variously the "launch bar", or "start bar" or "bar start". This is a metal bar which is adjusted for the safety of competitors. This is based on observations in practice runs and trials prior to the main competition.

cherry trout: the spotless salmon is a breed of Japanese salmon known as the cherry trout.

FIS: Fédération internationale de ski et de snowboard (The International Ski Federation).

Dr Walter-Hofer: a legend in the world of ski-jumping, widely celebrated for popularising the sport. Walter-Hofer is the former FIS Race Director (now retired).

Japanese iron sparrow: this is a literal translation from the Norwegian. In English this species of songbird is called the Japanese Pygmy Accentor and is found throughout Japan and near Busan on the South Korean peninsular.

Kuzuki woodpecker: also known as the Japanese Pygmy Woodpecker is native to Southern Japan. The name "kuzuki" in Japanese means something close to "harmony", "peace", "brightness" and "hope".

Zakopane: a ski-jumping hill in Poland also known as Wielka Krokiew.

Raggsock: a type of sock popular in Scandinavia, sometimes referred to as 'ski socks' in the UK also raggsocks and 'ragg socks' (rare).

Jan Boklöv: Swedish pioneering ski-jumper whose struggles to keep his skis parallel in the 1980s led to his discovery that the V-shape formed in ski jumping was an advantage. The V-style known as the Graf-Boklöv technique has since been adopted across the sport and increases lift underneath ski-jumpers in flight. This reduces airspeed and substantially improves the distances a jumper can achieve.

bobcat: a lynx and an American company specialising in mowers and excavators, a frequent feature around North American ski jump stadia.

Hakuba Ski Jumping Stadium: in Japan was host to The Winter Olympics 1998. This was the third time, the then 25 year old Noriaki Kasai had competed at the Olympics. Noriaki Kasai set the world record for distance here in October 1993 with a 126.5 metre flight.

Harrachov: Following his close battle at the Winter Olympics on home turf in 1998, Noriaki Kasai went on to compete at Čerťák a stadium in the town of Harrachov in the Czech Republic, winning the 1998 World Championships. Kasai had won on the Flying Hill six years previously, in 1991-92 at the age of just 19 years old.

Kulm: host to five Ski Flying World Championships, Noriaki Kasai won the FIS Ski Jumping World Cup on the Flying Hill here in 2013-14.

K-point: From the German *Konstruktionspunkt* is the point a skier must cross in order to obtain points and is sometimes called "the calculation line" or "the k-spot".

kveldsrenn Kuusamo: Ruka in Kuusamo, Finland is a ski jumping and winter sports ground. It was here where Kasai flew 145 metres, winning the Individual Large Hill Final. The video on YouTube is worth seeking out, to see Kasai performing one of the most elegant and heart-stopping jumps of his career. Kveldsrenn here means "race" which is the correct term in Norwegian, so an alternative reading this poem would be to see Noriaki in competition with the sun.

grankonglene: In Norwegian the concept of a "king" is embedded in the idea of pine cones. Here Noriaki is seen as the king of the treetops.

Funaki, Harada, Okabe, Saito, Kasaya: refers to ski jumpers that have all competed for Japan both before during and after Noriaki Kasai (Kazuyoshi Funaki, Masahiko Harada, Takanobu Okabe, Hiroya Saitō and Yukio Kasaya).

g-spot: The spot at which all energy from the approach is gathered to the maximum point of momentum, prior to springing from a jump, as well as the perhaps more familiar meaning.

Kollen: Holmenkollbakken the site of the first ski jump in Norway in 1892. The first jump was constructed from chopped trees piled high with snow. It wasn't until 1952, when the Winter Olympics came to Oslo that a permanent structure was built for spectators to watch all the action.

hoppukas / Ski Jump Week: the name for the eight day World Cup competition in which ski jumpers participate in events also Norwegian for "hopscotch".This competition is known variously as Vierschanzentournee, The Four Hills Tournament and German-Austrian Ski Jumping Week.

Vikersund: Vikersund Hill or Vikersundbakken where Kasai placed 3rd in 1998, and both times in 2015 and 2016, before a breakthrough silver in 2017.

Bischofshofen: The German-Austrian Ski Jumping Week (see also *hoppukas*) takes place annually in Bischofshofen. According to the FIS's own website, "in 2000 the judges' tower was blown up" thankfully by demolition experts, with the intention to build a brand new one, which they since have, alongside an impressive K125 hill. Kasai competed here in 2016, three weeks before the birth of his daughter, Rino.

Yatzy: Not quite the same as the game sold in shops, this is the Scandinavian original using dice, paper, pencil and luck.

22,000: The crowd capacity at Zakopane, Poland.

Hornindalsvatnet: Literally "Hornindals Lake". Hornindalsvatnet is the deepest lake in Europe as well as home to a ski jump nestled among the pines.

Mühlenkopfschanze: In Willingen, Germany. In 2013 public funds were raised for a refit by selling bricks from between 20 to 1,000 euros a piece to those willing to help support the construction of the new Hessen Ski Jumping Tower. Kasai jumped here in 1999, achieving 132.5 metres and claiming first place.

Planica: In Slovenia in 2016, Noriaki Kasai completed his 500th individual competition in the World Cup against stiff competition.

ACKNOWLEDGEMENTS

Our thanks and appreciation to individuals and organisations who have supported our work on this translation including: Aaron Kent and Stuart McPherson, Geir Nummedal, Flamme Forlag, Jo Nesbø, The Stephen Spender Trust, Norwegian Literature Abroad, The Royal Literary Fund, The Royal Norwegian Embassy, Newcastle University's SELLL (School of English Literature, Language and Linguistics), NCLA, Jennifer Essex, New Writing North, Snowsport England, SJ Fowler, W. N. Herbert, Viva Tertulia, Ros Wynne-Jones, Matt Bryden and Nikita Lalwani.

LEGG UT UROEN DIN

Milton Keynes UK
Ingram Content Group UK Ltd.
UKHW030748061024
449258UK00004B/117